Original title:
Waves and Wonders

Copyright © 2025 Creative Arts Management OÜ
All rights reserved.

Author: Ophelia Ravenscroft
ISBN HARDBACK: 978-1-80581-563-1
ISBN PAPERBACK: 978-1-80581-090-2
ISBN EBOOK: 978-1-80581-563-1

Triton's Lament

Oh Triton, with your trumpet loud,
You blow to chase away the crowd.
But fish now laugh at your great horn,
While mermaids tease you, feeling scorn.

Your seaweed beard's a tangled mess,
And crabs invest in new dress.
You chase them down, but they all flee,
Deep down you're quite the sight, you see.

Beyond the Breaking Point

Surfboards balance on a joke,
As clumsy riders start to croak.
They tumble down like tangled leaves,
The shore just laughs, no one believes.

Seagulls giggle as they steal fries,
From beachgoers lost in the skies.
You try to shout, but the sand flies,
Beware the tides, they're full of lies.

The Lullaby of Distant Shores

A lullaby sung by a crab,
As it pinches all who aren't drab.
Oh sleepy sun, it sets too quick,
While jellyfish dance a cheeky trick.

The tide rolls in, a sneaky foe,
Stealing shoes, what a splashy show!
But laughter fills the salty air,
As seaweed wigs twirl everywhere.

Fluid Fantasies

In the swim, a fish might grin,
At the sight of its own fin.
A dolphin leaps with a playful jest,
While tourists go on a wild quest.

The sea shimmies with a cheeky charm,
As the tide works up its own palm.
A splash, a gasp, a sudden slip,
Life's a ride on a wondrous trip.

Secrets Beneath the Surface

Bubbles pop with a squeaky sound,
As fish wear glasses, quite profound.
Crabs do a tango, shuffling in time,
While clams recite poetry, oh so sublime.

Starfish in flip-flops, strut with glee,
Playing cards, sipping seaweed tea.
A dolphin jokes with a silly grin,
Tickling turtles for their next win.

Rhythm of the Roiling Sea

The tide must have heard a funny joke,
As seagulls laugh, it's quite the hoax.
Octopuses juggle underwater cans,
While barnacles gossip about bands.

The surf is jiving, what a sight!
Mermaids dance in neon light.
A whale plays sax, oh what a tune,
Under the glow of a cheese-shaped moon.

Breezes of Infinity

A gust blew by, tickling noses,
Sending sea urchins into poses.
The wind whispered secrets of tickly fun,
As kites danced above, under the sun.

Pelicans dive with a belly flop,
While sand crabs jump and never stop.
A breeze that giggles, a brisk ballet,
Is this the best beach day? I'd say yay!

Dancing Fluctuations

The shore sways like a drunken friend,
As splashes giggle, they just won't end.
Fish doing the cha-cha, seals applaud,
  While jellyfish juggle, oh how odd!

The horizon winks with a cheeky smile,
  It's partying hard, let's stay a while.
Shells whisper secrets, oh what delight,
Every flip brings laughter, joy, and light.

Resplendent Reflections

A fish in a tuxedo, quite the sight,
Swimming with jellybeans, oh what a delight!
Seagulls wearing sunglasses scream with pride,
While crabs are building castles, yes, they reside.

Shells are gossiping secrets, all very loud,
As starfish dance circles, feeling quite proud.
With bubbles as balloons, they rise and they pop,
In this underwater party, it's hard to stop!

Mysteries on the Horizon

A pirate with pancakes sails to the east,
Searching for syrup, oh what a feast!
His parrot keeps squawking, 'map it on toast!'
While fish play charades, they honor their host.

The sun wears a sombrero, splashes of cheer,
While dolphins on surfboards glide without fear.
A treasure of laughter, tucked under the sea,
What a strange place for a breakfast jamboree!

The Salty Serenade

Mermaids in tutus sing silly songs,
While octopuses play ukuleles along.
The clams keep the beat with a clapping of shells,
And sea cucumbers waltz, oh, how it dwells!

Turtles in bowties roll in the sand,
With crabs as their sidekicks, oh isn't it grand?
A conch shells the chorus, a laugh with a cheer,
In this salty soiree, good times are near!

Crystalline Echoes

Icebergs wearing hats glide with such grace,
While penguins in tuxes race in a chase.
A polar bear juggles with fish on a spree,
His friends cheer him on, come watch, you'll agree!

Snowflakes drift down, all twirling and spry,
Each landing like confetti from a bright sky.
The frosty air giggles, who knew it could be?
A wintertime circus, oh, what a jubilee!

Beneath the Crystal Canopy

Bubbles rise with a silly pop,
Fish wear hats, they never stop.
A seaweed dance, a jelly jig,
Under a shell, a crab sings big.

Starfish play cards, the stakes are high,
Octopus juggles as dolphins fly.
Turtles race with a hasty swim,
While seagulls cheer with a joyful whim.

A clam declares, "I'm the king!"
Crabs verse each other, let's have a fling!
With every flip, a splash of joy,
The ocean's games, a giggling ploy.

Oceanic Illuminations

Glowworms sparkle in the deep night,
Sea cucumbers dance in the moonlight.
A clownfish wears a polka-dot tie,
While shrimp fly by with a gummy sigh.

The anglerfish gives a bright grin,
As lanterns sway, let the fun begin!
A narwhal twirls, so fancy and spry,
While squid do tricks, oh my, oh my!

Coral reefs throw a disco bash,
With dancing mollusks, a splashy splash.
Whale calls echo like doo-wop fun,
Together they laugh, their joy well-spun.

Harbor of Hidden Truths

In a bay where secrets like to sit,
A goldfish whispers, "I've got the wit!"
The pelicans gossip, very loud,
While krill sneak by in a giggling crowd.

Seagulls swoop with a cheeky flair,
While crabs play poker without a care.
A wise old turtle shares a bad pun,
With laughter echoing, they've only begun.

A bottle drifts, it's got a note,
"Who knew learning could be so remote?"
The jellyfish read it, topsy-turvy,
While turtles laugh 'til they get dizzy.

Lullabies of the Lagoon

A sponge sings softly, a lullaby tune,
While frogs croon sweetly beneath the moon.
The starry night holds a whispering breeze,
As fish chase dreams with gentle ease.

Croaking frogs in a melodious spree,
Make bubbles rise in symphonic glee.
A sleepy shrimp dreams of a taco feast,
While the lagoon hums like a happy beast.

Crickets join in with a chirping song,
As the night creatures sway, they belong.
And underneath, where the bubbles play,
The lagoon hums softly, "Stay, oh stay!"

Whispers of the Deep

In the ocean, fish wear hats,
Sipping tea and chatting chats.
A crab plays tunes on a shell,
While seahorses dance quite well.

Jellyfish float on whims so grand,
With umbrellas made of sand.
They gossip 'bout the tides they see,
While dolphins giggle, full of glee.

Octopus juggling, what a sight!
He trips and falls, oh what a fright!
But then he laughs, no worries fuss,
In the depths, there's always us.

When night falls, the stars come out,
Making fish spin and shout.
In this deep, odd world we roam,
Such silly fun feels like home.

Ebb and Flow of Dreams

Turtles in scooters zoom on by,
With goggles on and the sun up high.
They race the pelicans in flight,
While starfish cheer with all their might.

A fish in a suit makes a speech,
About how far we'll swim and reach.
While seaweed stands up for a clap,
And the crabs outdo it all with a tap.

The seashells gossip, oh such a fuss,
As clams start giggling, throwing a bus.
Their bus ride dips, but they don't care,
In this realm, laughter fills the air!

A whale blows bubbles, what a show,
While clowns in the depths put on a glow.
Each ripple brings a smile anew,
In this life under skies so blue.

Serene Swells of Discovery

Upon the shore, a starfish pranced,
While crabs in tuxedos danced.
They twirled and whirled with such delight,
Teaching the seagulls to take flight.

Anemones play peek-a-boo,
While clownfish dress in vibrant hues.
They've got a party every night,
Where sea snails join in for a bite.

A diver trips, oh what a splash,
While playful otters make a dash.
With surfboards made of driftwood tight,
They glide and giggle, pure delight.

On sandy shores with laughter loud,
We find our fun amidst the crowd.
With every splash and quirky sight,
The ocean's secrets feel so bright.

Surges of Serenity

A pelican's hat flew high and wide,
While dolphins made it a fun ride.
They flip and flounder with such zest,
A feathered friend on their quest.

Sea cucumbers rolling, oh what grace,
With sea urchins watching, keeping pace.
They giggle as they tumble down,
Creating joy without a frown.

A pirate fish says, 'Arr, me mate!',
While clam pirates dig for a plate.
They feast on pearls with silly grins,
As krill join in, tossed into spins.

When the sun sets over waves so wide,
They dance in colors, side by side.
In this whimsical world, we find,
The joy and laughter intertwined.

Chronicles of the Coast

At the shore, a crab takes a stroll,
Wearing sunglasses, pretending he's cool.
He dances and prances, oh what a sight,
While seagulls complain, they're losing the fight.

A dolphin flips over, shows off its flair,
While fishermen gasp, tossing bait in despair.
With a splash and a giggle, it leaps out in glee,
Who knew the sea had such wild irony?

Breaths of the Blue

A fish in a tux plays a grand violin,
Jellyfish tango, spinning on a whim.
Octopus drummers keep everyone in time,
As starfish cheer loud, all clapping in rhyme.

The seaweed sways like it's part of the band,
As crabs get down, their moves oh so grand.
With bubbles of laughter, the deep sea glows,
Even the blind sharks smile at the shows.

Cascades of the Curious

A clam plays hide-and-seek with a ray,
"Catch me if you can!" it shouts in dismay.
But the ray just floats, relaxed in its space,
"I'd rather nap, you silly old face!"

Turtles tripping over their flippers in haste,
Snapping selfies, what a silly waste!
While a fish comments, "On land that's a chore,"
But in water, it's laughter — who could ask for more?

Infinite Ripples

A hermit crab changes its home on a whim,
Trying on shells that are shiny and slim.
His friends roll their eyes, "You look rather strange!"
But he just grins wide, "Aren't you glad I changed?"

An otter floats by, munching a snack,
With seaweed in hair, it's quite the attack!
As waves of laughter ripple through the crowd,
They cheer for their friends, loud and proud!

Capturing Distant Echoes

In the splash, a fish does dance,
With a jump that's quite the prance.
Seagulls squawk, what a funny sound,
As they chase chips that hit the ground.

Old boats drift with a creaky groan,
They whisper tales of the unknown.
Fishy friends beneath the glass,
Gossiping 'bout the folks that pass.

Tides tickle toes with a gentle tease,
Making splashes that bring us to knees.
A crab in shorts, oh what a sight,
Scuttling sideways, ready to bite.

So we laugh at the ocean's jest,
And cherish moments we love the best.
For in this dance, we find delight,
Even when the sun sets out of sight.

The Surf's Unseen Stories

A dolphin flips with a splash and grin,
Gossiping with seaweed and kin.
Shells whisper secrets, oh so sly,
Covering truths that swim on by.

An octopus wearing a funny hat,
Waving hello as we just chat.
The sun sets low, it starts to sway,
While sand crabs join the dance and play.

An old beach ball rolls, lost from the crowd,
It giggles softly, feeling quite proud.
As the breeze tells jokes to the salty air,
We chuckle together, without a care.

And when the tide pulls back with flair,
Footprints vanish, but moments we share.
In this realm of dreams, we feast,
On laughter that never will cease.

Curly Qs in the Sand

We build a castle, oh so grand,
With turrets made from grainy sand.
But then a wave, with a playful shove,
Sends it crumbling; oh, how we love!

A seagull lands, looks rather vain,
Pretending he owns the whole terrain.
With a strut and hop, he claims his prize,
While sand tries to tickle his little thighs.

Kids make patterns, curly Qs abound,
They laugh and tumble, joy unbound.
A buried treasure? Just some old shoes,
Shiny and bright like candy in hues.

So let's twirl and play, forget the sun,
For in this playground, we're all just fun.
We dance with the tide as friends unite,
Making memories from morning to night.

The Heartbeat of the Brine

The ocean hums a silly tune,
As sea turtles dance beneath the moon.
A fishing boat, in a wobbly ride,
Shares a laugh with fish on the side.

The tide rolls in with a playful sigh,
And sand flies up, oh my, oh my!
While starfish giggle and dolphins play,
The sun dips low, ending the day.

A crab named Frank with a big red claw,
Claims he's the king; we just guffaw.
With jokes so bad, they make us swoon,
We join him laughing 'til the night's maroon.

So here we gather, all in a line,
Sharing giggles as waves intertwine.
For every splash and every grin,
Forms the heartbeat of our kin.

Echoes of Eleutheria

In a land where seagulls play,
A fish wore sunglasses all day.
It danced on the beach with flair,
Leaving footprints without a care.

Crabs held a talent show at dawn,
While the starfish practiced to yawn.
They all applauded with tiny claws,
Silly antics without a pause.

A turtle rode a surfboard sleek,
And made the dolphins giggle and squeak.
The jellyfish juggled seashells bright,
Every splash brought more delight.

As the sun set on this funny scene,
The water glimmered, oh so keen.
With a wave of a fin, they took a bow,
A comedy troupe, who knew just how.

Nautical Narratives

Out on the sea, an octopus sings,
While balancing treasures like strange bling.
He tells tales of sailors lost at sea,
While jellyfish bob like they're carefree.

A pirate parrot squawks with fright,
Claiming the kraken is out tonight.
But it turns out, it's just a whale,
Who swam too close with a soggy tail.

A lobster with a monocle reads,
A newspaper filled with fishy deeds.
"Shark steals sandwich!" It made quite a fuss,
As the clam laughed and waved hello to us.

With a flick and a splash, they all unite,
To share laughs and jokes into the night.
Under the moon, their giggles soar,
In a world where the sea tells jokes galore.

Curls of Cosmic Energy

At the beach, the stars start to shine,
The waves dance wildly, looking divine.
A crab in a cape takes a grand leap,
While laughter from fish makes the sea leap.

The sun made a sandwich, so rude,
It forgot to put in some good food.
While the moon rolled its eyes in the sky,
Said, "When's lunch?" with a cosmic sigh.

Ocean currents declared a parade,
Where sea cucumbers donned a charade.
With floats made of shells and bright seaweed,
They all giggled, feeling quite freed.

As the night tickles this salty space,
Starfish giggle and join the race.
In the whirlpool of joy, they all gleam,
Under the cosmos, a silly dream.

Secrets of the Shoreline

Hidden treasures lie beneath the sand,
A flip-flop's lost, it takes a stand.
Shells whisper tales of old-time fun,
Making up legends, one by one.

A pelican juggling jellybeans,
Meanwhile crossing off funny routines.
His bill was a stage, his feathered flair,
Audience of crabs became more than rare.

A hermit crab dressed in a top hat,
Did a waltz with a fish, imagine that!
They twirled and spun with giddy glee,
Drawing laughter from the salty sea.

As sunset paints the beach in gold,
The creatures share stories, cheeky and bold.
With secrets of laughter in every tide,
Life on the shore is a joyful ride.

Enigmas of the Ocean's Depths

In the deep, a fish wears a hat,
While a starfish sings to a plump stray cat.
Crabs in tuxedos dance all night,
Thinking each shell is a disco light.

The octopus thinks he's a master chef,
Cooking up noodles, oh what a mess!
Seahorses giggle in their tiny homes,
While jellyfish juggle with spaghetti bones.

Turtles race in a slow-motion trance,
With seaweed wigs, they prance and dance.
A whale in a wetsuit, what a sight,
Searching for treasure in the pale moonlight.

Mermaids hold parties in coral reef halls,
Serving up snacks from the ocean's malls.
With laughter and magic, they twist and twirl,
In the depths of the sea, there's a curious whirl.

Labyrinths of Lapping Waters

A fish with glasses reads a book,
In a sea of bubbles, come take a look.
Clams play chess on a sandy shore,
Arguing rules, oh what a bore!

Frogs in suits hop into the scene,
Debating who's the ocean's queen.
With each little splash, they make quite the fuss,
As they try to catch a passing bus.

Dolphins wearing caps sing off-key,
Performing for crowds, just wait and see.
A pirate with socks mismatched and torn,
Claims he's the bravest, though he's quite worn.

In whirlpools of giggles, the creatures play,
Inventing new games to brighten the day.
With humor afloat and spirits so bright,
These ocean escapes bring delight and light.

Celestial Currents Above

In the sky, balloons take flight,
Chasing clouds like birds in sight.
The sun spills lemonade on the ground,
While giggles of rainbows drift around.

Stars play hopscotch in the dark,
They missed some squares—oh, what a lark!
Planets spin in a silly dance,
Tripping over their cosmic pants.

The moon's a cookie, bright and round,
But crumbs of dreams float all around.
Comets slide on banana peels,
While stardust makes them squeal with feels.

Galaxies laugh with glittery puff,
Shooting stars out, not yet enough!
In this sky of whimsical delight,
Every sparkle bursts in laughter's light.

Currents of Curiosity

A fish wore spectacles, quite a sight,
Reading seaweed in the soft moonlight.
Turtles play chess on the sandy floor,
While lobsters plan a dance encore.

Octopuses juggle with ocean weeds,
Pufferfish write books about their seeds.
Clownfish crack jokes that tickle the sea,
Making everyone giggle with glee.

Seahorses wear tiny hats, so smart,
Sipping tea from a conch for a start.
They toast to the jellyfish's great feat,
Who moonwalks on waves with gooey feet.

With bubbles that burst into laughter's song,
Curiosity swims where it belongs.
In a splash of antics, a finned parade,
Every twist twirls a new escapade.

Tides of Enchantment

A hermit crab lost its shell on the shore,
Wearing a thimble, it cracks up the floor.
Starfish audition for a Broadway show,
With legs so wiggly, they steal the glow.

Crabs in tuxedos dance a cha-cha,
While anemones sing, 'Ha! Ah, ha!'
The tide rolls in with a tickle and tease,
As sea cucumbers join with the breeze.

Seashells gossip under the sun's beam,
Sharing secrets in a salty dream.
Mermaids laugh at their glittery scales,
While dolphins spin like joyful tales.

Every flip and flop brings smiles about,
Embracing the joy with a joyful shout.
In this world, where enchantment plays,
Each bubble bursts with whimsical jays.

Ripples of Reverie

A turtle dreams of open skies,
While sipping nectar from a flower prize.
Fish tap dance on the ocean floor,
Creating ripples of laughter and more.

Seagulls play tag with drifting boats,
And sing silly songs with funny notes.
The tide returns with a splashy grin,
Sending starfish in a high-flying spin.

Seashells spin tales of long-lost ships,
With seaweed crowns on their tiny lips.
Crabs recite poems about their day,
In the most delightful and wacky way.

When the sun sets, all colors blend,
Bringing forth joy that seems to extend.
In this realm of imagination's flight,
Every ripple giggles, then takes its night.

Fluid Fantasies

The ocean's a jester, making us laugh,
With seashells that sing and fish that dance craft.
A crab in a tutu, a starfish in shades,
Invites us to join in spontaneous parades.

A dolphin flips jokes, flips and flops too,
As sea cucumbers nod, like they're laughing with you.
A whale calls your name, but it's hard to hear,
Could be he's just mumbling, having a beer!

Old turtles on surfboards take wild slides,
While jellyfish giggle on the ocean's tides.
They tickle the fancies of those who come near,
Beware of the sea, it's a place full of cheer!

Under the sun, all the sea critters play,
With fishy confetti celebrating the day.
So come, dip your toes in this hilarious sea,
Where fun is the current that sets laughter free.

Tranquil Tides of Time

In a hammock made of algae, I sway and I rock,
While fish tell bad puns through the old coral dock.
A seagull complained, 'My sandwich is fried!',
As crabs snickered softly, 'You'll just have to abide!'

Time drips like molasses, slow and absurd,
While octopus poets pen lines unheard.
A clam rolled its eyes at the sun overhead,
'Why do we always argue? Just eat instead!'

Starfish lounge middle, picking up sand,
While turtles debate whose turn is to stand.
'In this timeless void, let's just have a meal',
Fish chips on the side; what a moment to seal!

Waves giggle and tango in their frolicsome way,
While humor swims freely through the milky bay.
If laughter's your compass, then come take a ride,
For the sea is a jest, and it won't run dry!

Spirals of Saltwater Stories

In the depths of blue, tall tales take flight,
With seahorses spinning under moon's silvery light.
A shrimp spins a yarn 'bout the net that he dodged,
While a fish winks in jest, 'That's a buffet I lodged!'

Whales share words, like an epic sea show,
While currents weave punchlines we barely know.
'Why don't fish play piano?' a sole asked aloud,
The answer flopped back, 'They're just too proud!'

A grouper in glasses reads a sea-sprayed book,
While pirate crabs plot, but they're hooked with their look.
Stories twist like shells, in a loop and a curl,
With laughter the currency, let it unfurl!

So gather around, let the currents amuse,
With tales of the sea, you simply can't lose.
Reel in the fun, let's create and concoct,
For every good frolic is never quite blocked.

Melodic Marshes

In a swampy duet, frogs croak with delight,
As fish in tuxedos swim past on their flight.
A snail plays a trumpet made out of a shell,
While the turtles dance fast—oh, they do it so well!

Cattails gently sway, keeping time with the breeze,
As creatures all gather, doing spirals with ease.
Bobcats keep beat, moving paws over toes,
In a swamp-full of laughter, even mud clogs the nose!

The crickets provide the rhythm of cheer,
While bullfrogs break rhythm, but we keep them near.
In the marshland fiesta, it's all about fun,
Where laughter is thick, like the shine of the sun!

So if you feel low, come join in the play,
In these melodic marshes, we dance the day away.
With friends from the swamp, every moment's a blast,
Telling our jokes, let our silly things last!

Secrets of the Abyss

A fish wore a hat, it looked quite grand,
It wiggled its tail, trying to take a stand.
A crab played the drums with a shell on its lap,
While a starfish sang songs in a one-piece wrap.

The octopus danced with a flair of surprise,
In shoes made of seaweed, under the skies.
He tripped on a turtle who huffed with disdain,
Then they both had a laugh as they rolled in the rain.

A dolphin in glasses read jokes from a book,
The punchline made everyone give a quick look.
They chuckled so hard, bubbles filled the air,
While mermaids just giggled, flipping their hair.

In the depths of the blue, there's a party indeed,
Where fish wear bow ties, and sea urchins lead.
With laughter and bubbles, fun never goes dry,
In the world down below, come on and give it a try!

Twilight's Caress on the Coast

The sun took a dip, its rays turned to toast,
A crab had a party and claimed to be host.
With shells piled in mounds, like a banquet so nice,
Even jellyfish joined, oh, but not for the rice!

A seagull in shades tried to rap on the sand,
It fluffed up its feathers, thought it was quite grand.
While the barnacles grooved on a rock with some flair,
The waves whispered secrets, or maybe a dare.

Starfish performed with such twists and such spins,
While the porpoise cheered, tossing in some fins.
As crabs lost their footing and tripped on the beach,
They laughed till they dropped, just out of reach.

Twilight's embrace jested with joy in the air,
Shells ringing like bells, with no single care.
The coast celebrated till the stars took their place,
With a dance and a chuckle, in this magical space!

The Spell of the Sea Breeze

A seahorse slipped on its fanciest dress,
Swirled in the currents, feeling quite blessed.
It boogied with eels, all tangled in fun,
While waves shared a joke about riding the sun.

Sand dollars chuckled, their jokes pretty dry,
They rolled and they tumbled, oh my, oh my!
A clam by the shore shouted, "Hey, what's the deal?"
"Did you hear about the fish that learned how to wheel?"

The sea breeze came drifting with tickles and cheer,
It tangled their hair, oh how they did steer!
A crab in a tutu sang loud with delight,
As the gulls flapped around and jumped in the night.

In the depths of the fun, there's a rhythm, a rhyme,
With crustaceans and fish, making beats every time.
Their laughter and giggles floated under the moon,
A spell of pure silliness that ended too soon!

Luminescence of the Night Sea

The moonbeam waltzed on a mirror of blue,
While fishes in pajamas danced two by two.
A lanternfish glowed, thinking it was a star,
While dolphins gave high-fives from distances afar.

A whale played peek-a-boo with a big splash,
While squids had a paint party, creating a splash.
Their colors did whirl in a mad, joyful spree,
As jellybeans floated, tiny jellyfish glee.

The seashells chimed in, harmonizing sweet,
With beats of the ocean, making fun sound complete.
As plankton did twinkle like holiday lights,
Drawing guests from the depths on those magical nights.

In the night sea's glow, joy swirled in the air,
With laughter and giggles, there's happiness to share.
So come join the fun where the jokes never cease,
In the sparkle and shimmer, find your heart's peace!

Dance of the Liquid Mirage

Bubbles pop, a fishy joke,
As seaweed twirls in a merry folk.
Crabs wear hats, and laugh in glee,
Even the oysters shimmy, you see!

Flip-flops flop, a slippery chase,
Seagulls gossip with style and grace.
The tide rolls in, making a fuss,
As jellyfish sway without a bus.

Sandcastles rise, then they collapse,
While surfers flail in their bold mishaps.
Fiddler crabs dance, so full of cheer,
On a beach that's wild with laughter here!

The sun dips low, the day is done,
Yet the beach keeps partying, oh what fun!
With sunsets painted in giggles galore,
Life's a beach, who could ask for more?

Echoes of the Shoreline

The tide comes in, whispers and squeaks,
Starfish chat, wearing funny beaks.
Sand is flying, a dog's playful start,
It thinks it's Picasso, oh what a part!

Seagulls steal chips, and cluck with glee,
While kids build forts, thinking they're free.
Ocean's laughter rolls in like a song,
As waves play tricks, it won't be long.

Shells are treasures, or's that a shoe?
What's lost in the surf might still feel new.
Crabby comedians, they crack a grin,
While the water tickles our toes and chin!

With every crash, the shoreline leans,
Where laughter shimmers, and joy convenes.
Each splash tells a tale, alive and bright,
In this quirky dance, hearts take flight!

Reflections in the Sea's Mirror

A seagull swoops, steals a snack,
Then dances away, in a feathered act.
Fish flip-flop in a comical spree,
Splashing about, aren't they just free?

Mirrors of salt and a splash of fun,
Sandy toes race–who will outrun?
The treasure hunt reveals a lost shoe,
How many laughs can they fit in a view?

The sun winks down, what a silly sight,
As dolphins wear sunglasses, feeling all right.
A crab on a surfboard, what a thrill,
Attempting to balance, with style and skill!

As shadows grow long, the shore's alive,
With giggles and splashes, watch them thrive.
In this sea of chuckles, never a bore,
Each reflection shows us there's always more!

Chasing the Horizon's Glow

Kites fly high, a colorful blaze,
While winds blow whispers in playful ways.
Sea turtles bumble, it's quite the sight,
Swimming around like they're full of light!

Sandcastles giggle, their towers so tall,
Until a brave wave makes them all fall.
Lobsters in shorts, a style so grand,
With shells that shine from the sun-kissed sand!

Chasing sunsets, a race so wild,
Flip-flops in hand, like a carefree child.
Surfboards surfing on the crest of fun,
Packing joy in this dance under the sun!

As twilight blankets the bustling shore,
The laughter lingers, who could want more?
With stars winking down, the night's aglow,
As memories splash, in a joyful flow!

Currents of Enchantment

A fish in a suit swam by with a grin,
His tie was too tight, a definite sin.
He asked for a dance on the ocean floor,
But tripped on a jelly, and out he did soar.

The crabs played some tunes with their claws in a band,
While starfish all clapped with a soft, sandy hand.
But one crab got stuck in the conch of a shell,
He bopped to the beat but he couldn't yell, 'help!'

Seahorses giggled, they jumped over rocks,
Chasing bubbles and bits from the lunch of the flocks.
A dolphin in moonlight did twirl and did spin,
But lost his cool shades, oh, where to begin?

With laughter they danced as the tide swept along,
Each splash held a note, a bubbly song.
The ocean's a stage for silly, sincere,
With laughter and joy all the critters cheer!

Serenity in the Swell

In a sandcastle kingdom, the buckets were grand,
A sand crab declared, 'This is my homeland!'
He wore a crown made of seashells and clay,
'The king of the beach!' he would proudly say.

A seagull looked down, gave a snicker and squawk,
'You think you're a monarch? You're just a beach rock!'
The crab puffed up, said, 'I'll prove that I reign!'
But slipped on a wet spot, and fell on his brain!

With starfish advisors all gathered around,
They debated the best way to turn it around.
'Perhaps a new hat!' suggested a clown,
'Or maybe a paddle to take on the crown!'

They packed him with shells, gave him fish for a snack,
Determined to help their dear king get back.
And there on the shore, they had giggles galore,
For kings are just crabs, and who could want more?

The Whisper of the Deep

A clam held a secret it swore it would share,
But when it was time, it just changed the hair.
'If clams can have curls, then why can't I?'
The octopus thought, with a wink in his eye.

He borrowed some kelp, adorned with a bow,
And danced through the sea like a strange underwater show.
But tripped on a sponge and got tangled in green,
Now looked like a salad, a curious scene!

The turtles swam past, and they chuckled with glee,
'Fashion advice? You're not free as a bee!'
And lobsters in suits with their claws held up high,
Proclaimed, 'In the deep, you always must try!'

So back to the clam, he crawled with a flair,
And said with a grin, 'Who needs all the hair?'
For style in the sea is a funny old thing,
And laughter, not hair, makes a clam truly king!

Celestial Ripples

The moon sent her light like a dance on the tide,
A starfish who twinkled felt bliss, oh, so wide.
He spun in a circle, a graceful ballet,
While octopi cheered from the depths far away.

A comet drew pictures, like swirls in the deep,
But a turtle with stars just wanted some sleep.
He yawned wide and long, disrupting the view,
And ended up snoring as he floated on through.

The fish joined the dance but forgot all the steps,
They flailed and they flopped, leaving jellyfish perplexed.

With laughter, they tumbled and swirled in delight,
Creating a ruckus as day turned to night.

As the cosmos glittered, they swam without care,
For friendships in ocean are treasures so rare.
In the depths of the sea, where the silliness reigns,
The stars sparkled down like shiny, happy chains!

Beneath the Surface's Smile

Beneath the surf, fish play hide and seek,
With a shrug and a wink, they dance and sneak.
A crab in a hat, oh what a sight,
Dancing on sand, exaggerating its height.

Seagulls caw loudly, but no one can hear,
The tales of a clam, with nibbles of beer.
Starfish gossip on the sandy floor,
Trading tall stories they couldn't ignore.

The octopus chuckles, ink spilling with glee,
Scribbling love letters for all to see.
While turtles can't stop with their silly old tricks,
Playing tag with seaweed, oh what a mix!

So join in the laughter, let merriment rise,
For below, in the currents, the humor lies.
Every shell tells a story, in spirals they spin,
Life's a jest in the deep, let the fun begin!

Melodies of the Salted Air

The breeze has a dance, pirouetting free,
Tickling the noses of the folks by the sea.
A sea otter hums while munching a shell,
Singing off-key—it's a charming rebel!

Seashells are drummers, thumping the beat,
While a jellyfish wobbles, like it can't find its feet.
Whales whisper secrets, making the waves sway,
With fin-flipping jelly, they brighten the day.

The sun winks down, adding sparkle and flair,
As dolphins do flips, without any care.
So laugh with the wind, sing silly and spry,
For nature's a stage, under the vast sky!

This salty symphony, full of glee,
Tells stories of joy, so let it be.
With each and each note, make spirits soar high,
Leave worries behind, like clouds passing by!

Tide Pools of Imagination

In puddles of wonder, the sea stars frolic,
With crabby applause, their antics are comic.
A sea cucumber giggles, no cares in the world,
While barnacles boast, their secrets unfurled.

There's a snail in a shell, boasting it's fast,
But all of its friends know it's a slow, funny cast.
The seaweed orchestra sways to its tune,
Composing sweet ballads, beneath the moon.

A fish in a top hat, quite dapper and grand,
Juggling small seashells with a flick of its hand.
Meanwhile, anemones dance in delight,
Tickling the toes of those who come by night.

In these tiny worlds, where laughter flows free,
Magic abounds in each splash of the sea.
So dive in with glee, let imagination take,
For silliness thrives in each oceanic wake!

Horizons Unveiled

With a flip of the fin, the horizons unfold,
Revealing the tales of the brave and the bold.
Schools of fish gossip about the day's fun,
While octopi chat, eyeing the sun.

A treasure chest giggles, full of old gold,
Chased by a seagull, a story retold.
The anchored boats bob, as if in a race,
Cheering for crabs who run with such grace.

Bubbles rise swiftly, like laughter in air,
While sea turtles smile with their slow, gentle flair.
As dolphins jump high, splashing like sprites,
An ocean of humor dancing in sights.

So gaze at the horizon, let joy set sail,
In a world where laughter is bound to prevail.
For life on the coast is a comedic chase,
Join in the magic; it's a silvery place!

Driftwood Diaries

A piece of wood floats on by,
Its journey planned by the sky.
It says, "I'm here for a ride!"
While seagulls laugh, full of pride.

It dodges fish, goes left and right,
Winks at the sun, oh what a sight!
Crabs take bets on its next play,
While jellyfish drift on ballet.

With barnacles dressed like bling,
It claims it's the driftwood king.
Bobbing in glee, it's no fool,
A ruler of the sea's cool pool.

But as the tide begins to rise,
"Is this my end?" the driftwood cries.
With a splash, it meets the shore,
And humbly whispers, "Just one more!"

Harmony of the Horizon

In the distance, a line so neat,
Where sea and sky joyfully meet.
Sunbeams dance in a silly caper,
As boats glide past like a happy paper.

Clouds play hide-and-seek in blue,
While dolphins giggle, "What's new with you?"
Tickled by breezes, they leap and twirl,
Making waves that shimmer and swirl.

With seagulls singing their goofy tune,
An octopus choruses, "Give us a moon!"
Jellyfish float with a bob and a sway,
Making sure they steal the whole show today.

At sunset, they gather for a feast,
With barnacles served as the main beast.
Laughter echoes as shadows play,
In a world that's bright in a comical way.

Embrace of Ebbing Currents

As the tide recedes with a chuckle,
Sandy feet wiggle, oh what a shuffle!
Shells whisper secrets, quite hilarious,
"Don't be a clam, be more gregarious!"

Crabs play tag, all in a rush,
"Catch me if you can!" they say with a hush.
Starfish giggle, spread out with flair,
"Look at us now, we're everywhere!"

With slippery fish donning a grin,
Sneaking up close for a swim.
"Is this a game?" one fish suggests,
"Let's make a splash, we're on a quest!"

As the sun dips low, colors blend,
The sea winks back; it's all pretend.
In the embrace of silly streams,
Life is fun, just like our dreams.

Celestial Reflections

The moon grins down, a cheeky sight,
As stars begin their comic flight.
"Catch me if you can!" they call in glee,
Twinkling bright on the singing sea.

Seashells gossip on the sandy shore,
"Did you see that star? Oh, what a bore!"
As crickets chirp their nightly tune,
A raccoon joins, saying, "Now that's a boon!"

Inky waves rippling, soft and silly,
Creatures laugh, while the night feels frilly.
"Join our party!" they all invite,
As the cosmos winks with pure delight.

With a splash from below, a fish takes flight,
Dancing with bubbles, oh what a sight!
Under moonlit skies, they all rejoice,
In this cosmic comedy, hear their voice!

Oscillations of the Soul

A fish put on a tiny hat,
Swam by a crab who wore a spat.
Together they danced a silly jig,
While jellyfish joined, in costumes big.

The ocean floor held tea parties bright,
With starfish serving cakes of light.
A parrotfish tried to sing a tune,
But sounded more like a big raccoon.

Seahorses played hopscotch on the sand,
While dolphins threw confetti, oh so grand.
A whale brought bubbles instead of cake,
And all the sea critters began to shake.

So when you think of ocean cheer,
Remember the antics that disappear.
Beneath the surface, there's much to see,
Laughing with creatures, wild and free.

Undersea Revelations

An octopus lost its shiny shoe,
In a game of hide and seek with a blue.
The clams began to giggle and cheer,
As the turtles snickered, 'It's over here!'

A crab, with a monocle, gave a wink,
"Lost something, my dear? Come have a drink!"
With coral cocktails and seaweed snacks,
They laughed till the sun fell through the cracks.

A mermaid flipped her shiny hair,
Declared, "I found a treasure rare!"
But it turned out to be a lost balloon,
That floated away, singing a tune.

In the depths where laughter resides,
The sea holds stories that it hides.
Join in the fun, take a dive down,
Where silliness reigns with a seaweed crown!

Echoes in the Abyss

In the deep where the shadows play,
A narwhal snorted at a stray ray.
They formed a band with a conch shell drum,
And bubbles danced like a shimmying hum.

A sing-song crab offered jokes galore,
While fish laughed till they were sore.
"Why did the anglerfish cross the line?
To catch a selfie in the sunshine!"

An engineer sea cucumber tried to build,
A submarine made of seaweed, thrilled.
But it sank as a shrimp blew a kiss,
Resulting in underwater bliss.

With every giggle that rang through the sea,
Echoes of joy, so wild and free.
Remember these tales when you feel blue,
For the ocean has laughter waiting for you!

The Ocean's Embrace

A seal folded laundry with much ado,
While clowns of the sea juggled a shoe.
Anemones waved in a friendly way,
Whispering secrets of a bright day.

The star-studded sky held a fishy glow,
With the deep-sea dancers stealing the show.
A pufferfish puffed up with pride,
Saying, "I'm the best, none can hide!"

Squids drew pictures in flowing ink,
While penguins slipped, all tried not to sink.
A laugh erupted from a whale so grand,
"Join me, friends, in this comedy band!"

So if you're ever feeling grey,
Just listen to what the sea critters say.
In their embrace, joy takes its place,
And the heart finds a home in this merry space.

Celestial Dance of the Surf

The moon wears shades, a stylish sight,
While stars giggle, shining so bright.
Fish breakdance in their ocean show,
And crabs join in, with a delightful glow.

Seagulls perform their aerial trick,
Squawking jests while picking up sticks.
Dolphins laugh at their own splash,
As jellyfish glide, quite a splashy bash.

The sun turns pink, a clown at noon,
While seaweed twirls in a funky tune.
A sandcastle stands, all wobbly and grand,
As seashells giggle, oh, isn't life grand?

And as the tide pulls back in surprise,
A starfish grins, no need for disguise.
With all this fun on the ocean's floor,
Who needs a land when you've got folklore?

Eternal Entanglements

A turtle forgot where he left his snack,
As sea urchins laugh, giving him slack.
With each little wave, a new tale unfolds,
Of crabs in bow ties, so stylish and bold.

An octopus juggles shimmering shells,
They giggle with glee, like they know all the spells.
A plankton parade floats by in delight,
While mermaids roll their eyes at the sight.

A fish in a tux shimmies with flair,
While sea cucumbers sulk, too flat to care.
With barnacles cracking jokes on the rocks,
The ocean's a circus, just don't wear socks!

With every splash, there's laughter to find,
The currents' sweet secrets, so wondrous, unkind.
In this watery world where hilarity grows,
Just keep swimming, and let the fun flow!

Veils of the Verdant Sea

In greenish gowns, the kelp likes to sway,
While fish play tag, in a bubbly ballet.
A pufferfish pouts, not wanting to play,
While shrimps huddle close, giggling away.

Anemones wave like they'd won a race,
While crabs, always late, just shuffle with grace.
The coral reefs whisper sweet jokes at dawn,
As fish wear their best, all spruced and drawn.

Nudibranchs prance with colors so bright,
While a clam tells a tale of the last moonlit night.
It's a never-ending jest, this sea-side affair,
With laughter and bubbles, floating in air.

So join the antics, take a goofy dive,
Where the ocean's humor comes alive.
In slick little splashes, the day will unwind,
And you'll leave with a smile, laughter entwined.

Quest of the Quicksilvery Tide

The tide tickles toes, with a gleeful tease,
While crabs scuttle off, just trying to sneeze.
A treasure map drawn with seaweed and sand,
Leads to giggles and snacks—oh, isn't it grand?

Starfish hold meetings, their pointy discussions,
As dolphins discuss their latest combustions.
Seagulls provide commentary, feathers all fluffed,
While sandcastles sit, feeling quite gruffed.

A sardine parade swims in perfect sync,
While a clam shakes his head, "What do you think?"
With a wink and a splash, the tide moves in fast,
This oceanic quest is a blast, unsurpassed!

So let's ride the bubbles, with joy and a chime,
As fish spin tales, defying all rhyme.
In a world that's alive with chortles and cheer,
The quest down below is the best kind of sphere!

Secrets of the Salt Unknown

The ocean's secret's quite a tale,
Where crabs wear hats and fishes sail.
Seagulls gossip, with a caw,
About a whale who's lost a straw.

In salty air, the quirks abound,
As mussels growl and otters sound.
A dolphin dances, all in glee,
While sea cucumbers sneak some tea.

A clownfish tells a joke so grand,
It leaves the starfish all unmanned.
The tide laughs hard, a bubbling cheer,
As barnacles break into a beer.

Underwater parties, quite a sight,
Where shrimp do the tango, oh so tight.
The ocean hums a playful song,
Of sea creatures who just sing along.

Constellations in the Current

The stars are fish who swim at night,
In cosmic pools, their scales so bright.
Octopuses wear the crown of stars,
While crabs dream of cars and guitars.

Anglerfish light up the dark,
Like disco balls that make a spark.
The jellyfish glide in rhythmic dance,
Wiggling their jellies, given a chance.

A stargazer swims with an astrological map,
While the turtles take a classy nap.
An eagle ray swoops down low,
To join the party with a joyful flow.

Tides create laughter, rolling in,
Where starfish are the judges, let the fun begin!
They declare a winner with a flip and a spin,
Under the moon's gaze, let the silliness win.

Portraits of the Pulsing Sea

In the gallery of water, what do we see?
A jelly in a wig, oh what a spree!
The fishy faces sport the best grins,
While the clowns take selfies with their fins.

A striped bass strikes a pose so fine,
Next to the seahorse, sipping on brine.
"Cheese!" says the starfish with perfect flair,
Capturing moments without a care.

The conch shells whisper secrets of brine,
About a hermit crab with a taste so divine.
Each portrait matched with a punny name,
As the giggles of dolphins ignite the fame.

"Sea-esta" signs hung on coral reefs,
Where laughter swims as everyone thieves.
The fish cheer loud, it's a photoshoot,
With bubbles and smiles, it's all so cute!

Serenity in Shifting Sands

On sandy shores, where footprints flee,
A crab creates art so carefree.
He scuttles left, then scuttles right,
Painting dunes under the moonlight.

The wind tells tales, a giggling breeze,
As seagulls jockey for the best cheese.
Sands shift careers, from hourglass to beach,
They tick and tock, just out of reach.

Turtles stroll with style, oh so slow,
While fish in jackets put on a show.
The sandcastle's guard, a brave snail knight,
Defends its towers with all his might.

Chasing crabs, laughing along the shore,
As the tide plays tag and always wants more.
Each grain's a giggle, in the sun's warm band,
In this quirky paradise of shifting sand.

Beneath the Surface of Dreams

A fish in a top hat, quite the sight,
Swims in circles, hoping for a bite.
He talks to the crabs, and they laugh with glee,
Sharing tales of the sea, oh what a spree!

A dolphin with shades struts the ocean floor,
Singing pop tunes, always wanting more.
Seashells are DJing a shimmering beat,
Grooving the sea otters, they're hard to beat!

A squid with a quill writes a bestseller, too,
About underwater dance-offs and a crew.
With ink as his palette, he colors the night,
While starfish are judging, it's quite the sight!

So dive in, dear friend, to this circus of fun,
Where jellyfish jump and all finish a pun.
Life with a splash, a tickle, a tease,
Underneath your dreams, it's a comic breeze!

Chasing Liquid Echoes

A seal in a cape chases whispers of sound,
Bouncing off bubbles, joyously unbound.
His friends wave goodbye, as he leaps from the blue,
In pursuit of a giggle, he's truly on cue!

An octopus juggles bright pearls from the sea,
Each toss is a laugh, what a sight to see!
With eight wiggly arms, he dances with flair,
While crabs clap their claws, showing they care!

A whale dons a wig, just for the show,
Belting out ballads that steal the flow.
His notes cause a splash, a gurgle delight,
Echoes of laughter ringing through the night!

So dive into mirth, let the chuckles arise,
In this world of mischief, there's no need for sighs.
Stories of splashes and giggles take flight,
With every new ripple, heart full of light!

Cosmic Caresses

A starfish in moonboots dances with grace,
Twinkling in rhythm, lighting up space.
Meet comets that wobble, with tails made of cheer,
As they spin and they swirl, bringing joy far and near!

An alien fish, with a hat made of gold,
Tells tales of adventures, wild and bold.
He jests with the planets, they chuckle in sync,
Splashing in stardust, they sip on a drink!

A nebula floats, painting skies with a grin,
Wiggling and giggling, letting the fun in.
Shooting stars zoom past, with jokes up their sleeve,
In this cosmic dance, you won't want to leave!

So put on your shades, and come join the spree,
Where cosmic delights are as wild as can be.
With laughter that sparkles, and joy that transcends,
These celestial frolics will never see ends!

Rhythms of the Rising Tide

A crab in a band, clasps his claws and vows,
To rock out the rhythm, under seaweed brows.
He strums a sea cucumber, it hums with a tune,
As fish crowd the dance floor, beneath the bright moon!

Anemones bounce, in a wavy parade,
Twisting and twirling, they're not afraid.
They cheer for the conch with its horn made of shell,
Blowing out laughter, casting a spell!

A shrimp plays the spoons, keeping beat with a smile,
While starfish, in sequins, dance all the while.
They shimmy and shake in this underwater bliss,
Where every move's magic, a whimsical kiss!

So let's catch the tide, in this frolicsome ride,
With giggles aplenty on this joyful side.
The rhythms are flowing, the laughter's set free,
In the ocean's embrace, come giggle with me!

Tides of Discovery

The sand went flying as I ran,
A seagull squawked, a true cartoon fan.
With buckets and shovels, we searched in glee,
Finding old cans and a rusty key.

The key went 'clink' and then 'splash', oh dear,
Was that a fish that just grinned with cheer?
I laughed so hard, I lost my hat,
Now it's a home for the jolly fat cat!

A jellyfish wobbled, doing its dance,
I tried to impress with my best wave-prance.
Instead, I slipped and went down with a flop,
Now I'm a model for the seaweed shop!

The tide rolls in with secrets to share,
Like dad's old jokes—beyond compare.
When the sun goes down, and the stars do glow,
We dig for treasures, but find just a toe!

Undercurrents of Dreams

A crab in a tux, what a sight to behold,
He waved his claws, acting quite bold.
While watching a sunfish, so round and so true,
I wondered, should sushi come dressed up, too?

The octopus laughed, 'Join my ballet!'
'Not a chance,' I said, 'I've got a beach day!'
But there I went, swirling round with a spin,
Tangled in seaweed, it's a soft-feathered win!

A starfish named Harold told jokes with his pals,
While dolphins played tag, oh those cheeky mammals!
With every flip, they'd chuckle and cheer,
While I just chased bubbles—or maybe a beer!

As dusk crept in, with stars in the sky,
This beachy adventure made time fly by.
So if you find dreams washed up by the shore,
Just remember to laugh and then laugh some more!

The Rhythm of the Ocean's Breath

The sun tickles shells while they lie on the sand,
Peeking at crabs like they've got a new band.
As I croon softly to the turtles nearby,
They stared at me blankly, like birds in the sky.

A hermit named Larry gave me quite the stare,
With his new shiny home—does he even care?
He said with a grin, 'Please don't make a fuss,
But my live-in roommate is a bus!'

The waves made a rhythm, a silly old beat,
I stomped and I clapped, feeling so neat.
Then a whale yawned wide, and I lost my cool,
It's hard to keep dancing when you're splashed by a pool!

With laughter echoing, as the moon shines bright,
I won't forget this jolly old night.
I'll hum with the tide and forget about woes,
As the sea shares its giggles—nobody knows!

Secrets Beneath the Foam

With my trusty snorkel, I took a deep dive,
Searching for treasures, oh, how to survive!
But all I discovered was a flipped rubber shoe,
I guess it's a trophy, what can one do?

A clownfish appeared, cracking jokes all around,
Said, 'What's in the box? A lost hound?'
I thought to reply, with a grin and a wink,
But my snorkel filled up, oh! Time to rethink!

A treasure map floated, but it led to a pie,
So confused at the sea, I forgot to cry.
With whipped cream and giggles, I made quite a mess,
Now I'm the pirate of culinary distress!

As the tide took my crumbs, I couldn't help grinning,
For every misstep felt just like winning.
So here's to the secrets beneath the wild sea,
Where laughter is hidden and carefree can be!

www.ingramcontent.com/pod-product-compliance
Lightning Source LLC
Chambersburg PA
CBHW072132070526
44585CB00016B/1638